Inside My Body

Why Does This Bug Bite Itch?

Steve Parker

Raintree

Chicago, Illinois

www.heinemannraintree.com
Visit our website to find out more information about Heinemann-Raintree books.

To order:
☎ Phone 888-454-2279
💻 Visit www.heinemannraintree.com to browse our catalog and order online.

© 2011 Raintree
an imprint of Capstone Global Library, LLC
Chicago, Illinois

Edited by Kate de Villiers and Laura Knowles
Designed by Steve Mead
Illustrations by KJA-artists.com
Picture research by Mica Brancic

Originated by Capstone Global Library Ltd
Printed in the United States of America by Worzalla Publishing

15 14 13 12 11 10
10 9 8 7 6 5 4 3 2 1

Library of Congress Cataloging-in-Publication Data
Parker, Steve, 1952–
    Why does this bug bite itch? : skin and healing / Steve Parker.
        p. cm. — (Inside my body)
    Includes bibliographical references and index.
    ISBN 978-1-4109-4018-6 (hc) — ISBN 978-1-4109-4029-2 (pb) 1. Skin—Juvenile literature. 2. Wound healing—Juvenile literature. I. Title.
    QP88.5.P37 2011
    612.7'92—dc22
                                                2010024804

Acknowledgments
The author and publisher are grateful to the following for permission to reproduce copyright material: Alamy pp. **15** (© Friedrich Stark), **24** (© Cultura); iStockphoto pp. **9** (© modesigns58), **13** (© jo unruh), **14** (© Liza McCorkle), **16** (© sumnersgraphicsinc); Photolibrary pp. **4** (Image Source), **5** (Nordic Photos/Peder Sundström), **7** (Imagestate/Jorn Stjerneklar), **11** (imagebroker RF/Harry Hart), **18** (Phototake Science/CDC CDC/Jim Gathany), **21** (Image Source), **27** (Fotosearch); Science Photo Library pp. **10** (Anatomical Travelogue), **12** (David Mack), **22** (Custom Medical Stock Photo/John Callan); Shutterstock pp. **17** (© Sonya Etchison), **23** (© Quayside), **28–29** (© Andresr).

Photographic design details reproduced with permission of Shutterstock pp. **11**, **13**, **17**, **19** (© Isaac Marzioli), **11**, **13**, **17**, **19** (© Yurok).

Cover photograph of girl scratching mosquito bite reproduced with permission of Science Photo Library/A J Photo.

We would like to thank David Wright for his invaluable help in the preparation of this book.

Contents

Words that appear in the text in bold, **like this**, are explained in the glossary on page 30.

What Is Skin?

When other people look at you, what do they notice? They probably see your smile, your eyes, the way you do your hair, your clothes—and your skin.

Skin is your body's protective covering, like a natural all-over coat. It guards your delicate inside parts, such as your muscles and nerves, against all kinds of dangers, such as scratches, hot sun, cold wind, and insects that bite and sting.

🔍 **Skin and hair color vary from one person to another.**

🔍 **On the sole of a person's foot, the skin is up to 5 millimeters thick. A rhino's skin is 10 times thicker!**

Color of skin

Each person has his or her own skin color. This depends mainly on the skin color of the parents. If both parents have light skin, their children usually have light skin, too. Skin color also depends on how much a person has been out in strong sunshine. Staying out in the Sun for a long time temporarily darkens the skin.

Extreme body facts

How big is skin?

- If an adult person's skin could be laid out flat, it would cover about 2 square meters (22 square feet), which is about the area of a twin bed.

- An adult's skin is heavy, weighing as much as 5 kilograms (11 pounds). That weighs more than two bags of flour!

- Your own skin weighs about one-eighth of your whole body weight.

What Does Skin Do?

Skin has many different jobs and functions. The main ones are listed here. Can you think of any others?

Protection

- Skin keeps your insides in! It wraps around your soft inner parts and protects them from damage.
- Inner body parts contain liquids such as blood. Skin stops these liquids from drying up or leaking out.
- Skin prevents liquids from leaking in, such as rain or water from the bath, sea, or swimming pool. These liquids would harm the delicate inner parts.
- Skin keeps out dirt, germs, and other harmful substances.

SCIENCE BEHIND THE MYTH

MYTH: You only sweat when you're hot.

SCIENCE: Usually you sweat when you get hot, as part of skin's temperature control. However, if you are very worried or afraid, you may be sweaty even when cold. This is part of the body's natural "fight or flight" reaction in case you have to run away from danger. Fast running would make you very hot, but the reaction means that sweat is already there to keep you cool.

Temperature and touch

- When it is very hot or very cold outside, skin helps to keep the insides of the body at a regular, constant temperature. This is called temperature control.
- Skin provides your sense of touch, so you can feel things around you.

When it's hot, skin sweats to help the body stay at its normal temperature of 37 degrees Celsius (98.6 degrees Fahrenheit).

What Is Inside Skin?

Your skin may not seem to have an "inside," because it is on the outside of your body. However, if you could look very closely inside your body, you would be able to see the thickness of your skin. It has two main layers—the outer epidermis and the inner dermis.

Outer layer

The epidermis is constantly being rubbed by touching, washing, drying, wearing clothes, and many other activities. Yet it never wears away because it is constantly replaced. The epidermis makes more of itself, every minute of every day.

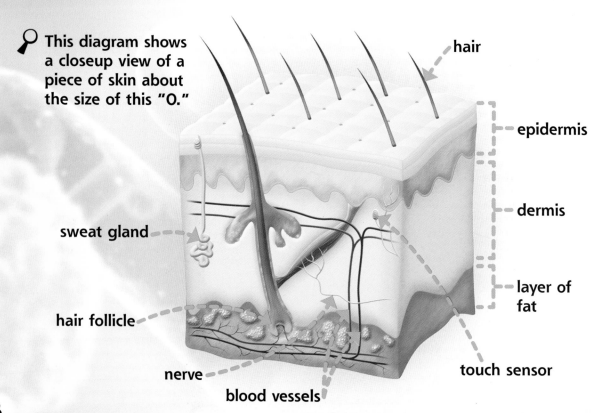

This diagram shows a closeup view of a piece of skin about the size of this "O."

hair

epidermis

dermis

sweat gland

layer of fat

hair follicle

touch sensor

nerve

blood vessels

Inner layer

Below the epidermis is a thicker layer, called the dermis. It contains millions of tiny nerve endings called **touch sensors**, which allow you to feel the world around you. It also contains blood vessels that bring nutrients to keep your skin healthy.

Beneath skin

Underneath skin is a layer of fat. This works like an all-over cushion against knocks and bangs. It also helps skin with temperature control by keeping in body warmth when it is cold outside and keeping out heat when it is very hot outside.

Skin gradually grows thicker if it is rubbed often. Gloves give extra protection for tough jobs.

Extreme body fact

Worn-away skin
If you could collect all the tiny flakes of skin that rub off your body every year, they would fill about five buckets!

How Does Skin Feel Touch?

Skin has millions of tiny parts called **touch sensors**, so that you can feel what comes into contact with your body.

Not so simple

Touch is not as simple as it seems. It varies from a light stroke to a painful knock. You know by touch if objects are hard or soft, wet or dry, cold or warm, smooth or rough. You can tell if they just brush against you or press hard on your skin. This is because skin has millions of touch sensors, of about six different kinds, each detecting a different feature of touch.

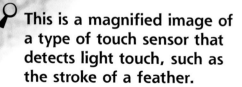

This is a magnified image of a type of touch sensor that detects light touch, such as the stroke of a feather.

No one has the same fingerprints as you. Every fingerprint on every person is different.

Fingertips

To feel something in tiny detail, you use your fingers. This is because your fingertip skin has the most touch sensors, packed very closely together. Fingertip skin also has tiny swirling patterns called fingerprints. These help you grip and pick up small items.

Practical advice

Hot or cold?

Fingers are great at detecting many things, but they are not so good at detecting hot or cold. That is why people sometimes dip their elbow into bathwater to check its temperature. If fingertips were very sensitive to hot and cold, this would interfere with feeling very small details.

Why Do We Wash Our Skin?

We need to wash our skin to keep it clean. If skin is not washed, it gets dirty and smelly and may develop spots and sores. As germs multiply on skin, they could cause serious illness.

When to wash skin

Most people take a bath or shower each day. But hands are always touching items that could carry germs. Because of this, it is best to wash your hands after using the bathroom, before each meal, and after handling dirty objects.

This image shows how germs (shown here in blue and green) collect on the surface of the skin, among body hairs.

SCIENCE BEHIND THE MYTH

MYTH: Blackheads are due to dirt.

SCIENCE: Blackheads are small pimples with dark centers. They are not always caused by dirt. They can form on clean skin, usually during the teenage years. Extra-careful washing may help to get rid of them. A pharmacist can advise on special skin washing products to help prevent blackheads.

How to wash skin

Make sure you wash your hands properly! Wet your hands, rub the soap in, and then rinse it off with clean water. Dry the skin with a clean towel or paper towel. Dirty towels put the germs back on your skin again.

Washing your hands helps to stop germs from spreading.

Practical advice

Skin allergies

Some people's skin is **allergic** to detergents for washing clothes. The skin becomes red, swollen, itchy, and perhaps breaks out. Special detergents that do not irritate the skin can be used to solve the problem.

What Are Freckles and Moles?

Skin is not the same color all over. Some people have small patches of skin that are slightly different colors. These patches are nearly always natural and harmless.

Freckles

The color of skin is due to a dark substance called melanin. Skin with lots of melanin is dark or black. Skin with little melanin is light or fair. Some people have small patches with slightly more melanin than the rest of their skin. These light brown areas are called freckles.

🔍 **If you have freckles, you might notice that they become slightly darker after you have been out in the Sun.**

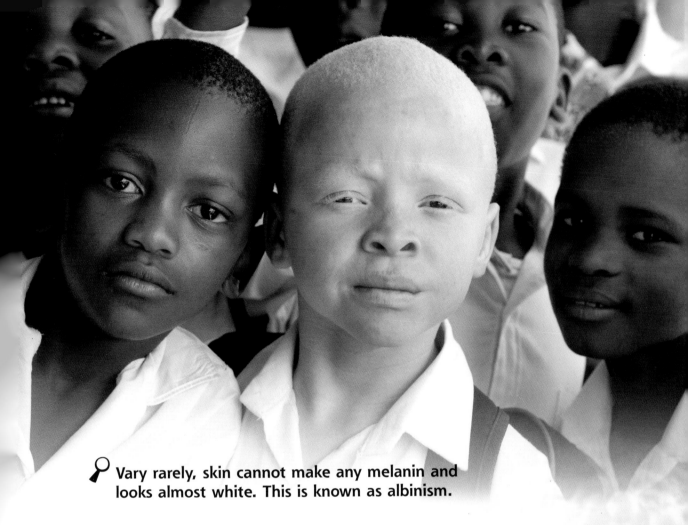

🔍 Vary rarely, skin cannot make any melanin and looks almost white. This is known as albinism.

Moles

A mole is a small patch of skin with lots more melanin, which makes it much darker. Moles are safe as long as they do not grow bigger, itch, become sore, or bleed. If this happens, check with a doctor.

Birthmarks

Birthmarks are colored patches of skin present at birth. There are several different kinds. Some are due to extra amounts of melanin, while others are caused by tiny blood vessels. Most birthmarks can be hidden with makeup or treated by a doctor.

What Does the Sun Do to Skin?

Skin protects your inside parts from all kinds of risks, including the Sun's rays. But too much sunlight can harm the skin itself, especially if the skin is light-colored.

Too much sun

Bright sunlight can be very harmful if it shines on skin that is not used to it, especially pale skin. If the skin becomes red, sore, and swollen, it has been burned by **ultraviolet (UV)** rays from the Sun. We call this problem sunburn.

Getting sunburned increases the risk of developing skin cancer, so avoid letting this happen.

Darker skin

If sunlight is not too strong, then over many days it makes skin gradually darken. This is called a suntan and is the skin protecting itself by making more melanin. But there are still risks, including **cancer**.

Practical advice

Avoid sunburn

- Avoid the Sun when it's strongest, between 11 a.m. and 3 p.m.
- Wear a hat and loose clothing to cover skin, especially during the middle of the day.
- Use a high factor sunscreen and follow the instructions carefully.
- Do not use tanning beds.

 SCIENCE BEHIND THE MYTH

MYTH: You can't get sunburned on a cloudy day.

SCIENCE: This is not true! On a hazy day, with thin clouds, the Sun's harmful rays can still pass through the clouds. You must still be careful to avoid getting sunburned.

What Hurts My Skin?

Many small problems cause skin damage, such as cuts, grazes, knocks, bruises—and pesky insects biting.

Why insect bites itch

A biting insect such as a mosquito stabs its needle-shaped mouth through the skin to suck up blood. As it does so, it squirts in a substance that stops blood from **clotting** (gettting thick and sticky). This means the mosquito can keep sucking. It later makes the bite turn into an itchy spot.

🔍 **This mosquito's body is filling up with red blood that it is sucking up through skin.**

Grazes and bruises

A graze is where the outer layer of skin is scraped away, showing the inner layer beneath. This needs covering with a bandage to stop germs from getting in. A bruise is where blood leaks from blood vessels inside the skin after a hard knock.

Impetigo

Bacteria cause several skin problems. Impetigo is a skin infection that causes red sore patches to appear, ooze fluid, and form yellow-brown crusts. Impetigo spreads easily to other people, so it needs to be checked by a doctor.

Practical advice

How to treat burns

If you get burned, tell an adult right away. Large or deep burns need urgent medical treatment. With any burn, you should seek medical advice.

- You should immediately put the burned area under clean, cold running water for at least 10 minutes.

- Loosely cover the burn with a sterile (clean) gauze bandage or plastic wrap to protect the burn from knocks and germs.

- Do not put creams, ointments, or adhesive (sticky) bandages on the burn.

How Does Skin Heal Itself?

After a small cut or graze, skin usually heals itself. A week or two later, it looks as good as new—because it is new!

Stages in healing

Skin heals itself in several stages.

- First, the leaking blood gets thick and sticky, to stop more blood from oozing out. This is **clotting**.
- The clotted blood gradually turns hard, forming a tough covering known as a scab.

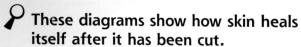 These diagrams show how skin heals itself after it has been cut.

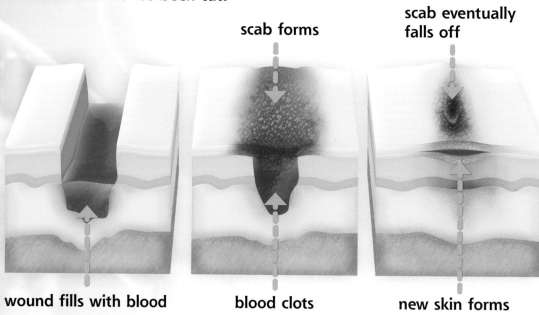

scab forms

scab eventually falls off

wound fills with blood

blood clots

new skin forms to close wound

- The damaged edges of the wound grow new skin across the gap, making the opening smaller.
- The skin edges grow together and close the wound.
- The scab shrinks, loosens, and eventually falls off.

It is essential to keep injured skin clean by washing it with an anti-germ substance called antiseptic, and to protect it from dirt and knocks with a clean bandage.

When healing goes wrong

Sometimes skin does not heal properly. There might be dirt or germs in the wound. The skin swells and turns red. There might be a throbbing pain and a pale yellow liquid called pus. A doctor will need to treat the wound.

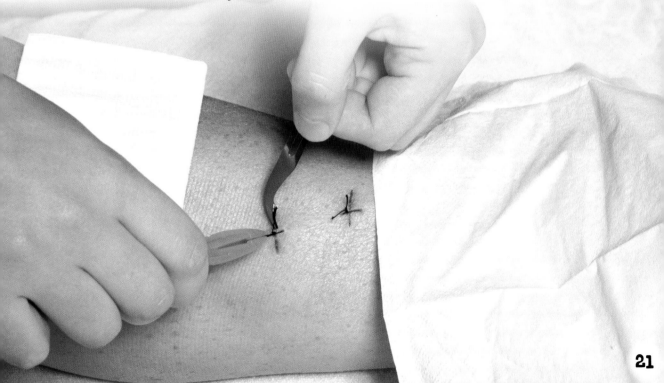

The edges of a deep cut can be held together with stitches or clips until the cut heals.

What Are Spots and Sores?

Many kinds of spots and sores can grow on skin. Most soon get better, but a few types should be shown to a doctor, especially if they do not start to heal after a few days.

Types of spots and sores

- A blister is a cushion-like mound of thin skin with clear fluid underneath that finally bursts. It is usually caused by too much sudden rubbing or by sunburn.

If your shoe rubs against your heel when you walk, it can cause a blister.

- A boil is a red, painful lump with a yellow, fluid-filled center or tip, where **bacteria** multiply in the skin. The yellow fluid is pus, a mixture of body fluids and bacteria. Usually the boil bursts and the fluid seeps out.

- An ulcer is a raw, sore area that can leak pale fluid. It can be caused by chemicals on the skin, too much rubbing, or infection with germs.

Treatment

These types of spots and sores need to be covered by a bandage for protection from knocks, dirt, and germs. This helps them to heal.

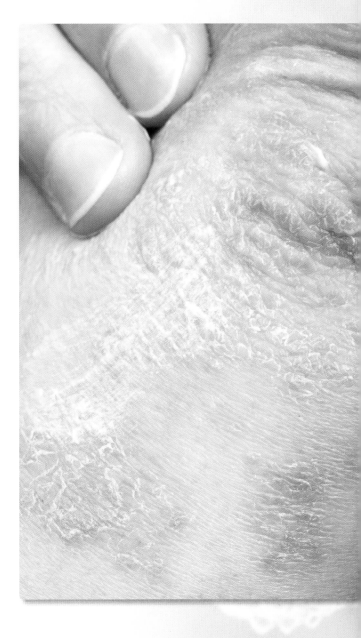

 Eczema is an itchy skin rash that can be treated with special creams.

SCIENCE BEHIND THE MYTH

MYTH: Fatty foods give you pimples.

SCIENCE: Foods do not usually give you pimples, unless you are very sensitive or **allergic** to them. Chocolates, cookies, and cakes do not make pimples more likely, but they are not good for your teeth and could make you gain weight.

How Long Do Hair and Nails Grow?

Uncut hair keeps growing for a few years and gets quite long. Usually the strands will then fall out and new ones will grow in their place. Nails keep growing without falling out, but as they get longer, they tend to crack, chip, and break.

🔍 **Hair can be curly or straight, thick or fine, and light or dark. What is your hair like?**

SCIENCE BEHIND THE MYTH

MYTH: Eating bread crust makes your hair curly.

SCIENCE: This is not true! You can make hair look different because you use hair straighteners or curlers, or dyes to change the color. But as the hairs grow at their bases, new hairs will grow in the same way as before. People's hair type is **inherited** from their parents and cannot be changed.

How hairs and nails grow

Hairs grow from tiny pits, called **hair follicles**, in the dermis layer of the skin. Each hair grows 2 or 3 millimeters each week. Eventually it falls out and a new hair grows from the same follicle. Hairs are made of the body **protein** known as keratin, which also forms nails and makes skin tough.

Nails grow from the nail root under the skin at the nail's base. The whole nail slowly slides along the skin beneath it, called the nail bed, and gets longer by about 1 millimeter each week.

Extreme body fact

Hair and nail records
- Xie Qiuping of China has hair more than 5.5 meters (18 feet) long. She's been growing it for over 30 years!
- The longest nails belonged to Lee Redmond of the United States. Her thumbnail measured 90 centimeters (35 inches) long!

How Can I Take Care of My Skin?

Each person's skin is different in color, thickness, and other features. But everyone's skin, as well as hair and nails, needs to be taken care of each day over the years.

Squeaky clean

Skin needs washing at least once every day. Otherwise it gets covered with dirt and old sweat, which soon start to produce the unpleasant smell called body odor. Most kinds of makeup do no harm, as long as they are washed off at the end of the day.

SCIENCE BEHIND THE MYTH

MYTH: Feet are very ticklish.

SCIENCE: This is true. If someone tickles the skin on the sole of your foot, you probably giggle. No one knows why. However, at the same time, you also pull away your foot. This would turn out to be a good idea if the tickle were really an insect ready to bite.

Older skin

As skin gets older it becomes thinner and less stretchy, and it starts to form lines and wrinkles. These can appear earlier in life if skin has been in bright Sun often or if the person smokes. Most of these skin changes are natural, and no creams or pills can stop them.

The skin of older people can become very wrinkly. Imagine what yours will be like after a lifetime of smiling!

Skin flakes
Every second, on average, about 500 tiny flakes of skin rub from your body. Most are lost when you dry yourself with a towel or do exercise. Much of the dust in houses is the skin flakes of the people who live there!

Skin, Hair, and Nail Facts

The eyelid and lip skin is thinnest, at just half a millimeter thick.

Most people have more than 100,000 scalp hairs.

Eyebrow hairs stop sweat from dripping into the eyes.

Skin lines form around often-used joints such as the finger knuckles.

There are more than two million tiny sweat **glands** in the skin all over the body.

Toenails and fingernails grow faster in summer than winter.

The least sensitive skin is on the lower back.

If you are right-handed, your right fingernails grow faster than your left ones.

The most sensitive skin is on the fingertips and lips.

The thickest hairs are eyelashes that keep dust out of the eyes.

Everyone's fingerprints are different.

Skin sweats most on the forehead, hand palms, foot soles, and under the arms.

Cold skin gets small lumps called goose bumps, which are due to tiny hairs standing up straight.

Glossary

allergic when a person's body is extremely sensitive to a substance that is normally harmless for other people and reacts against the substance with various changes, such as a skin rash

bacteria tiny living things that are found almost everywhere, including on skin. They are too small to see except under a microscope. Some types cause infection and disease.

cancer serious disease in which some cells in the body grow and multiply out of control

clotting when blood gets thick and sticky and stops flowing, usually when it leaks from a wound and comes into contact with air

gland body part that makes and releases a product, usually a liquid or oily substance such as sweat

hair follicle tiny pocket-like pit in the skin, from which a hair grows

inherit receive a body feature from parents, such as skin color or hair type. These features are determined by the genes passed from parents to offspring.

protein substance that forms many parts and structures inside the body, including skin and muscles

touch sensor microscopic part that responds to various features of touch such as light contact, hard pressing, heat, cold, movement, and pain

ultraviolet (UV) type of rays from the Sun, which we cannot see but that can harm the skin and cause sunburn

Find Out More

Books

Gray, Susan Heinrichs. *The Skin* (*Human Body*). Chanhassen, Minn.: Child's World, 2005.

Green, Jen. *Skin, Hair, and Hygiene* (*Your Body and Health*). Mankato, Minn.: Stargazer, 2006.

Websites

http://kidshealth.org/kid/htbw/skin.html

You can read some information-packed articles about skin at this website.

http://yucky.discovery.com/flash/body/pg000146.html

Learn more interesting facts about skin at this website.

www.kidsskinhealth.org/kids/index.html

Follow the adventures of Sammy the Skin Cell and learn about hair and nails, too, at this website.

Index